Original title:
Radiant Happiness

Copyright © 2024 Creative Arts Management OÜ
All rights reserved.

Author: Tim Wood
ISBN HARDBACK: 978-9916-88-232-0
ISBN PAPERBACK: 978-9916-88-233-7

Mosaic of Merriment

Colors blend and swirl around,
Laughter echoes, joy is found.
Each little piece, a story told,
In this bright mosaic, dreams unfold.

Sunshine dances on the floor,
Moments cherished, hearts will soar.
Together woven, spirits bright,
Merriment shines, a pure delight.

Glistening Hopes in the Air

Stars above twinkle and shine,
Wishes whispered, hopes entwine.
In every heart, a spark ignites,
Glistening dreams take glorious flights.

In a world where shadows play,
Hope breaks through, it finds a way.
With every dawn, a chance anew,
Glistening hopes, they guide us true.

The Lightness of Being Free

Wings unfurl, the spirit sings,
Into the sky, it simply springs.
Boundless fields, horizons wide,
In this lightness, we confide.

No chains to hold, no weight to bear,
In the moment, joy is rare.
Breezes whisper, they carry me,
Floating softly, being free.

Happiness Touched with Gold

Sunset hues in amber glow,
Moments captured, hearts in tow.
Laughter rings like chimes in air,
Happiness shines, beyond compare.

In every smile, a glimmer bright,
Touched with gold, pure delight.
With every hug and tender touch,
Happiness, we cherish much.

Serendipitous Smiles

In a crowded room, our eyes collide,
A spark ignites, where hearts abide.
Unexpected joy, a chance to find,
Serendipitous smiles, forever entwined.

Wandering paths, we softly tread,
Laughter shared, no words unsaid.
In fleeting moments, we discover grace,
A warmth that lingers, a sweet embrace.

The Art of Glowing Together

Hand in hand, through shadows we dance,
Creating a light, given half a chance.
In the stillness, our laughter hums,
Together we bloom, where joy becomes.

Colors blending, a joyous hue,
In every heartbeat, I feel you too.
As stars surround, our spirits soar,
The art of glowing, forevermore.

Joy Unfurled like Petals

Like flowers opening beneath the sun,
Joy unfolds gently, a day just begun.
With every whisper, the world feels bright,
Petals of laughter dance in the light.

In the breeze, our dreams take flight,
Colors vibrant, oh what a sight!
Embracing moments, deeply we trust,
In joy unfurled, our spirits combust.

A Canvas Painted with Laughter

On this canvas, colors collide,
Moments captured, with love as our guide.
Each brushstroke echoes a memory dear,
The laughter we share, a symphony near.

With every shade, a story unfolds,
In strokes of joy, our hearts are bold.
Together we paint, with dreams intertwined,
A masterpiece forged, in laughter we're blind.

The Symmetry of Happiness

In laughter's echo, joy takes flight,
Two souls find harmony, day and night.
With every glance, a spark ignites,
In shared moments, pure delight.

The sun may set, yet hearts are warm,
In love's embrace, we find our form.
Together, we dance through time's sweet song,
In the symmetry, we both belong.

Twinkling Eyes and Brimming Hearts

Twinkling eyes, like stars above,
Reflecting dreams and endless love.
Brimming hearts, with secrets shared,
In silent moments, we feel cared.

With every laugh, the world feels bright,
In simple joys, we chase the light.
Through gentle whispers, our souls align,
In this sweet bond, forever entwined.

Sweet Melodies of Togetherness

Softly strummed, the strings of fate,
In sweet melodies, we resonate.
Harmony wrapped in each embrace,
A symphony of love, fills the space.

With every note, our spirits soar,
In rhythms bright, we crave for more.
Together we sing, our voices blend,
In this grand journey, love won't end.

The Brilliance of Being

In the dawn's glow, life starts anew,
With every heartbeat, dreams pursue.
The brilliance shines in every part,
In just being, we feel the art.

Beneath the stars, our fears take flight,
In tender moments, everything's right.
Together we stand, united and strong,
In the brilliance of being, we belong.

The Joyful Pulse of Existence

In the quiet whispers of the night,
Life dances softly, bathed in light.
Each heartbeat echoes, a sweet refrain,
Joy blooms gently, like springtime rain.

Beneath the stars, dreams take their flight,
Hope ignites the dark, a dazzling sight.
Weaving through moments, a tapestry bright,
The joy of existence, our shared delight.

Love Letters to the Dawn

As the sun stretches, painting the sky,
Morning spills over, a tender sigh.
Whispers of love in the softest light,
Each dawn promising a new delight.

Birds sing sweetly a melodious tune,
Awakening hearts, like flowers in bloom.
Penning our dreams, with shadows of night,
In love letters stitched with dawn's gentle light.

Dancing in a Field of Sunflowers

Golden petals sway in the summer breeze,
Laughter erupts with every step and tease.
Under blue skies, we twirl and spin,
In fields of sunflowers, joy begins.

The sun smiles down, embracing the day,
With arms wide open, we frolic and play.
In the warm embrace of nature's song,
We find our rhythm, where we belong.

The Elixir of Happy Days

In laughter's glow, we sip the sweet cheer,
Moments together, loved ones draw near.
Bubbling joy in simple delight,
The elixir of life feels perfectly right.

With every smile, a potion we share,
Filling our hearts, melting burdens laid bare.
In the symphony of love, we sway and play,
Creating our magic, the elixir of days.

Celestial Smiles in the Sky

Stars twinkle bright, like eyes that gleam,
Clouds drift softly, weaving a dream.
Moonlight dances on whispers of night,
Embracing the world in gentle light.

A canvas above, painted so fine,
Each constellation, a story divine.
Galaxies whisper secrets to share,
In their brilliance, we find hope and care.

Silent wishes on shooting stars fly,
Heartfelt thoughts lifted high to the sky.
The universe sighs, a soothing embrace,
Celestial smiles, in timeless space.

Enchanted Echoes of Delight

In the forest where shadows play,
Sunbeams dance in a joyous display.
Birds sing melodies, sweet and clear,
Echoing laughter that tickles the ear.

Leaves rustle softly in the breeze,
Nature's whispers put the soul at ease.
Each moment a treasure, vivid and bright,
Enchanted echoes fill the twilight.

Winding paths lead us closer to bliss,
In every glade, a magical kiss.
Together we wander, hearts light as air,
Finding delight how the world can care.

The Glow of Weekend Wanderings

Sunrise breaks, a promise renewed,
Adventure awaits, hearts bright and imbued.
Footsteps echo on trails yet unknown,
In every step, a story is sown.

Laughter echoes through valleys and hills,
Finding joy in the moment that thrills.
Picnic blankets sprawled under the sun,
Sharing sweet memories, laughter, and fun.

As shadows grow long and daylight begins,
The world slows down, joy mingles with spins.
With loved ones beside us, time stands still,
Weekend wanderings, a keeper of will.

Warmth in the Chill of Night

Stars shiver softly in the frigid air,
Gathered 'round a fire, with stories to share.
Blankets wrap tightly, we huddle so close,
In the face of the chill, our warmth we'll boast.

The flames crackle, sending sparks to the sky,
Flickering lights that twinkle and fly.
Laughter speaks volumes, as shadows entwine,
Creating a bond that feels so divine.

In the night's embrace, friendships ignite,
A sanctuary found in the depth of the night.
Together we cherish this beautiful sight,
Finding true warmth in the chill of the night.

The Heart's Golden Hour

In twilight's glow, hearts entwine,
Golden beams of love, divine.
Whispers soft, moments shared,
Time stands still, feelings bared.

With every heartbeat, echoes bloom,
Promises linger, dispelling gloom.
Under the sky, dreams take flight,
In the heart's golden hour, all feels right.

Vibrant Paths Beneath Our Feet

Walking through life, colors blend,
Each step a journey, around the bend.
Footprints dancing on vibrant ground,
In every stride, new joys are found.

Nature's palette, rich and bright,
Guides us gently, day and night.
With every path, a story unfolds,
In vibrant hues, our future holds.

Illuminating the Darkest Corners

In shadows deep, light flickers near,
A guiding flame, we hold so dear.
With courage bold, we face the night,
Illuminating fears, bringing light.

Together we shine, hearts aglow,
With every spark, love begins to grow.
Through darkest times, we won't despair,
For in each other, warmth is there.

The Burning Bright of Connection

In the heart's fire, passions ignite,
Threads of friendship pull us tight.
Bound by laughter, love, and care,
In every moment, we boldly share.

Through trials faced, we stand as one,
Together we rise, as day is done.
With every heartbeat, bonds renew,
The burning bright of me and you.

Sunbeams Through the Window of Life

Sunlight filters through the glass,
Glimmers on the wooden floor.
Whispers of a peaceful moment,
Life's bright gifts we can't ignore.

Each ray dances with a purpose,
Warming hearts and lifting minds.
In the quiet of the morning,
Hope and light are intertwined.

Nature's canvas painted golden,
As shadows slowly drift away.
We embrace the warmth surrounding,
In stillness, find our way.

Through these beams, we glimpse the future,
A journey bathed in light so grand.
With each dawn, new dreams awaken,
A brighter world within our hands.

Illuminated Paths to Happiness

Every step upon this journey,
Guided by a gentle glow.
Paths illuminated softly,
Wherever we are destined to go.

Through the woods and over hills,
Dancing light guides us ahead.
With each choice, the heart fulfills,
In love, our worries shed.

The laughter shared along the way,
Reflects the joy we seek to find.
Together, we'll embrace the day,
Joy's light and peace entwined.

In moments filled with radiant grace,
We'll cherish what each path reveals.
Finding comfort in love's embrace,
Our happiness, the heart's ideals.

Bright Horizons of Love

Beyond the mountains, skies turn blue,
Where dreams of fondness take their flight.
In every glance, a world anew,
Awaiting at the break of night.

Hand in hand, our spirits soaring,
Through the clouds, where hopes arise.
With every heartbeat, love's restoring,
Painting sunsets in our eyes.

The horizon calls with sweet allure,
As stars emerge and softly gleam.
Together, our hearts will endure,
In this realm of shared esteem.

With love as vast as endless skies,
We'll chase the dawn, forever bold.
In every moment, passions rise,
A tapestry of dreams retold.

The Magic of Merry Moments

Laughter echoed through the air,
Moments wrapped in joy and cheer.
Each memory, a gem so rare,
Creating treasures we hold dear.

With friends gathered, hearts ignite,
Playful smiles and stories shared.
In fleeting time, pure delight,
In the magic, we are bared.

Dancing shadows in the twilight,
Echoes of our shared embrace.
Every twirl, a spark of light,
Capturing the essence of grace.

So let us dance through every hour,
Embrace this fleeting time divine.
For in these moments, love's sweet power,
Transforms the ordinary, aligns.

Sparkling Fragments of Joy

Bubbles rise in summer's light,
Laughter dances, spirits bright,
Moments caught like fireflies,
In the night, our heart's replies.

Children play beneath the trees,
Breezes whisper, soft as pleas,
Sunshine glints on morning dew,
Joy in fragments, always new.

Starlit skies and dreams take flight,
Memories woven, pure delight,
Every smile a glowing spark,
Lighting up the canvas dark.

In the quiet, love does bloom,
In every heart a tiny room,
Echoes of what once was here,
Fragments whisper, crystal clear.

The Rhythms of Happiness

Beats of laughter, hearts align,
Step by step, we weave the line,
Life a dance, so full of cheer,
In the music, moments near.

Sunrise paints the world anew,
Golden rays in skies of blue,
Waves of joy crash on the shore,
Every heartbeat wants for more.

Finding bliss in simple things,
In every smile, a song that sings,
Nature's choir, sweet and alive,
In its rhythms, we will thrive.

Harmony in day's embrace,
Every challenge, we will face,
Through the shadows, light will flow,
In the rhythms, we will grow.

Life's Brightest Chapters

Pages turn in soft-lit glow,
Tales of joy and tears will show,
Every lesson learned with grace,
In the journey, we find space.

Moments gathered, hands held tight,
Through the darkness, seek the light,
Every heartbeat, every sigh,
Marks the moments, passing by.

Chapters filled with dreams pursued,
Paths we walk, our thoughts imbued,
Laughter echoes, love's sweet art,
In these pages, paint the heart.

Life unfolds, a beautiful tale,
With every stumble, every trail,
Brightest chapters, boldly writ,
In the journey, we commit.

Serene Views from a Joyful Heart

Mountains rise in peace so grand,
Waves embrace the golden sand,
In the stillness, whispers flow,
From a heart that learns to glow.

Fields of flowers, colors blend,
Nature's canvas, sweet transcend,
Every breath, a moment cherished,
In its beauty, worries perished.

Stars above in night's embrace,
Silent wonders, timeless grace,
From the depths, our spirits soar,
In the quiet, we explore.

Harmony within the soul,
In each heartbeat, we are whole,
Through the lens of joy, we see,
Serene views, forever free.

Joyful Echoes

In the garden where laughter blooms,
Whispers of joy chase away glooms.
Every heart beats a happy song,
Together we dance, where we belong.

Sunrise paints the sky in gold,
Stories of hope begin to unfold.
Each moment, a treasure, pure and bright,
Joyful echoes in the morning light.

Uplifted by Serenity

Beneath the trees, a peaceful shade,
Nature's songs, in silence played.
Gentle winds caress the soul,
In this calm, we become whole.

Rippling waters, a soothing sound,
In quiet moments, peace is found.
Hearts let go of weight and strife,
Embraced by the beauty of life.

Days Brightened by Love

With every glance, the world ignites,
Love's warm glow through starry nights.
Hand in hand, we face the dawn,
In your eyes, my worries are gone.

Laughter dances like morning dew,
Every heartbeat whispers, 'I love you.'
Together we weave our dreams so bright,
Days are radiant, filled with light.

Sweet Serenade of Smiles

In the quiet of soft whispers shared,
Every smile is a secret declared.
Radiant moments, a joyful refrain,
Love's melody echoes like gentle rain.

Children's laughter, a sweet charade,
In every grin, memories are made.
Hearts aligned in this moment's style,
Together we bask in the warmest smile.

The Glitter of Heartfelt Dreams

In the silence of the night, they gleam,
Whispers of hope like a soft moonbeam.
Stars dance lightly in the velvet sky,
Painting dreams where our wishes lie.

Every heartbeat echoes a sweet refrain,
A symphony woven with joy and pain.
Through shadows we wander, hand in hand,
Creating a future, carefully planned.

Kaleidoscope of Contentment

Colors blend in a vibrant swirl,
Life unfolds like a soft, spun pearl.
Moments captured in joyous play,
Where laughter and love light the way.

Gentle breezes carry our sighs,
As we watch the clouds dance in the skies.
Every glance shared, a story told,
In this vibrant tapestry, we grow old.

Sunshine's Tender Caress

Morning breaks with a golden hue,
Wraps us softly, like a dream come true.
Birds rejoice in harmonious song,
Transforming quiet into a dance so strong.

Beneath the warmth of the glowing light,
Every shadow hastens its flight.
In the stillness, we find our way,
Guided by hope, we embrace the day.

Petals Kissing the Morning Light

Flowers bloom as the dawn arrives,
A tender scene, where beauty thrives.
Each petal opens, revealing its grace,
Unfurling layers in a gentle embrace.

Dewdrops glisten like diamonds rare,
A moment crafted with loving care.
Nature whispers in a language pure,
In this quiet magic, our hearts endure.

Wellspring of Warmth

In the quiet of dawn's embrace,
Gentle light fills the space.
Hope rises with the sun's ray,
Chasing the shadows away.

Hearts alight like flickering flames,
In the hush, we find our names.
Together we weave our dreams,
In this warmth, nothing seems.

Hands held tight, we walk along,
Singing softly, our hearts' song.
With every step, the world feels bright,
In the love that ignites the night.

Through the storms and the rain,
We find strength in joyful pain.
Every tear becomes a stream,
Flowing softly through our dream.

Heartbeats in Harmony

In the rhythm of whispered sighs,
Two souls dance beneath the skies.
With each heartbeat, a story told,
In the warmth of love's pure gold.

Like a melody soft and sweet,
We find comfort in our beat.
Every moment, a silent prayer,
In each glance, a world we share.

Through the chaos, we remain,
Melodies flowing like sweet rain.
Hearts entwined, forever bold,
In the harmony, we fold.

As shadows fade and daylight calls,
Together we rise, never falls.
In the music of life's embrace,
We find our home, our sacred space.

Sunlit Whispers of Joy

Golden rays peek through the trees,
Painting shadows in the breeze.
In this glow, laughter is found,
Joyful echoes all around.

Every moment shines so bright,
Chasing away the darkest night.
With a smile, we greet the day,
Sunlit whispers guide our way.

In the garden of dreams so rare,
Colors burst in fragrant air.
Each petal tells a tale of bliss,
In sweet silence, we reminisce.

As the sun begins to set,
Memories form, with no regret.
In the twilight, we stand true,
Sunlit whispers, me and you.

Laughter's Bright Embrace

In the spark of a shared delight,
Laughter dances, pure and bright.
With every giggle, a joyful cheer,
In these moments, we hold dear.

Through the trials, we find our way,
Bonded by laughter, come what may.
Echoes of joy fill the air,
In this embrace, nothing we spare.

Together we weave a tapestry,
Laughter's thread, a melody.
With each chuckle, a gentle breeze,
Joyful hearts, forever at ease.

In the warmth of this shared space,
Life shines through laughter's grace.
Hand in hand, we'll always stand,
In laughter's bright embrace, so grand.

Sparkling Moments

In the quiet of dawn's first light,
A whisper echoes, soft and bright.
Glistening dew on petals fair,
Each drop a story, beyond compare.

Children's laughter fills the air,
With joy that dances everywhere.
A fleeting glance, a smile shared,
Moments like these, we are ensnared.

Time stands still, just for a beat,
Life's little treasures, oh so sweet.
In the warmth of a gentle hug,
Sparkling moments, hearts are snug.

Memories captured, like fireflies,
Each one a twinkle in the skies.
Let's hold them close, let love ignite,
In sparkling moments, pure delight.

Horizon of Hope

Beyond the mountains, dreams still gleam,
A place where all our hearts can beam.
In the distance, colors blend,
A promise waits, around the bend.

With every dawn, the world awakes,
A chance to mend what often breaks.
Through clouds of doubt and fears unknown,
The horizon whispers, you are not alone.

Gentle breezes carry our sighs,
As faith ignites and sorrow flies.
Together we rise, hand in hand,
Towards the hope, a brighter land.

Let's chase the light, with every step,
Believe in dreams, and never rep.
In the vast expanse, we'll find our way,
A horizon of hope awaits the day.

Footprints in Sunshine

On sandy shores where laughter rings,
We leave our marks like feathered wings.
Each footprint tells a tale of cheer,
In sunshine's glow, we hold dear.

The waves will dance, they come and go,
But memories linger, like a flow.
Together we wander, side by side,
In every footprint, love won't hide.

Barefoot joy beneath the sky,
As seagulls call and breezes sigh.
In every step, a story unfolds,
Footprints in sunshine, tales retold.

Days will fade, but hearts remain,
In each imprint, we feel no pain.
So let us wander with joy aligned,
Footprints in sunshine, forever entwined.

The Radiance of Simple Pleasures

A cup of tea, the morning glow,
Soft music playing, sweet and slow.
In laughter shared, in stories spun,
The radiance of life has just begun.

A garden blooms, with colors bright,
Butterflies dance in sheer delight.
With every petal, joy expands,
In simple pleasures, love still stands.

A cozy fire on a winter's night,
Familiar faces, warm and bright.
We gather close, united by cheer,
In every moment, we hold dear.

The world may rush, but we will pause,
To savor life, just because.
In daily wonders, let's find measure,
In the radiance of simple pleasure.

Chasing Glimmers of Fun

We run through fields where laughter thrives,
Chasing glimmers beneath bright skies.
Every giggle paints the air,
In the joy of youth, we are laid bare.

With friends beside, the world feels grand,
Adventures waiting, a magic planned.
Through swings and slides, we take our flight,
In fleeting moments, hearts feel light.

When dusk descends and shadows play,
We share our secrets, dreams on display.
The stars above twinkle like gold,
In this tapestry of laughter, stories unfold.

Let's capture joy in every way,
In these glimmers, we long to stay.
May we hold tight to this fun we've spun,
Forever young, forever on the run.

The Light that Follows

In every step, a whisper glows,
A light that guides where the river flows.
Through darkness deep, it leads us home,
In shadows cast, we shall not roam.

When storms arise and fears take flight,
This steadfast glow becomes our sight.
With hope aflame, we carry on,
The dawn will break; the night is gone.

Each flicker dances, a beacon bright,
A promise kept, a warming light.
Against the odds, we stand as one,
With heart and spirit, we have won.

So take my hand, let's walk this path,
Through every challenge, every wrath.
In every heartbeat, this truth we borrow,
Love is the light, joy the tomorrow.

Cherished Moments Under the Stars

Beneath the vast and twinkling skies,
We gather 'round where memories rise.
Each star a tale, each wish a dream,
In this quiet place, life's magic seems.

We share our laughter, our hopes laid bare,
Time slows down in the gentle air.
With every glance, a story told,
Wrapped in warmth, in the night so bold.

The moonlight dances on whispered thoughts,
In these cherished moments, love's found and sought.
Hearts beat softly with the night's serenade,
In this sacred space, memories are made.

As night surrenders to the dawn's embrace,
We'll hold each moment, each gentle trace.
Forever grateful, we look above,
In the starlit sky, we find our love.

A Bouquet of Joyful Memories

A bouquet blooms in colors bright,
Each petal sings of pure delight.
From laughter shared to tears that sweep,
In joyful moments, our hearts do leap.

We walk through seasons of change and cheer,
Life's lovely tapestry woven here.
Each memory crafted, a fragrant grace,
In this bouquet, we find our place.

With every smile, a story grows,
In this garden, a love that glows.
The flowers flourish, come what may,
Through every storm, they find their way.

So here's to joy, both near and far,
In this bouquet, we find our star.
May we cherish every moment spent,
In the garden of life, love is our scent.

A Heart Full of Light

In the quiet of dawn's grace,
A warm glow paints the space.
Hope dances in the air,
With whispers of dreams to share.

Every heartbeat a song,
Where love and joy belong.
In shadows, warmth ignites,
A heart full of radiant lights.

With laughter, spirits soar,
Embracing what we adore.
Through every tear and smile,
We walk life's wondrous mile.

Together, we shine bright,
Guided by the starlit night.
As the world spins so fast,
We cherish moments that last.

Joy's Unfurling Petals

In the garden, colors gleam,
Nature's canvas, a sweet dream.
Petals open to the sun,
In the warmth, our hearts are one.

With each breeze that softly plays,
Joy unfolds in subtle ways.
The fragrance dances in the air,
A promise that life is fair.

As bees hum a gentle tune,
Underneath the silver moon,
We find bliss in every sight,
In the beauty's pure delight.

With laughter shared like gold,
In every moment, brave and bold.
Petals fall, yet hope remains,
In joy's dance, love sustains.

Symphony of the Heart

In silence, love begins to bloom,
Notes ascending, dispelling gloom.
A melody sweet and divine,
In our hearts, stars align.

Every rhythm tells a tale,
In the soft winds, we set sail.
With each beat, a story flows,
A symphony only love knows.

Together, we learn and grow,
In harmony, our spirits glow.
Through life's diverse refrain,
We find music in joy and pain.

With each echo, we embrace,
Every moment, a sacred space.
In the symphony, we unite,
Creating magic, pure and bright.

The Glow of Nature's Embrace

Underneath the towering trees,
Soft whispers stir with the breeze.
Sunlight dapples on the ground,
In this haven, peace is found.

Colors weave a vibrant tale,
As rivers sing and winds exhale.
Mountains stand with wisdom old,
Nature's glow, a sight to behold.

With every step, we find our way,
In the wild, we wish to stay.
Moments linger, soft and clear,
Nature's pulse, a rhythm dear.

In each sunrise, stories vast,
In every shadow, memories cast.
We embrace this gentle space,
In the glow of nature's grace.

The Warmth of Togetherness

In laughter, we find a glow,
Together, we let our spirits flow.
In shared dreams, we weave our thread,
In every moment, love is spread.

Through trials faced, hand in hand,
In each heartbeat, we understand.
With open hearts, we heal and grow,
In every hug, the warmth we show.

In quiet times, we find our peace,
In each other's eyes, worries cease.
In memories made, our anchors lie,
In togetherness, we touch the sky.

Through seasons change, our bond stays bright,
Together, we dance in soft moonlight.
In joy and sorrow, we find our grace,
In the warmth of love, we find our place.

A Canvas of Cheer

With every brushstroke, colors blend,
In laughter, we find our hearts extend.
On canvas bright, our dreams take flight,
In vibrant hues, we paint our light.

Each smile a shade, each laugh a line,
In moments shared, our spirits shine.
A masterpiece crafted side by side,
In joyful hearts, there's no need to hide.

With strokes of kindness, we create,
In every gesture, we celebrate.
A canvas where joy knows no end,
In every heartbeat, we transcend.

Together we art, in harmony sing,
In the canvas of life, we're everything.
Each color a story, every tone a cheer,
In this masterpiece, we hold dear.

The Glow of Grateful Hearts

In morning light, gratitude swells,
For simple joys, our heart compels.
With every breath, we pause and see,
In thankfulness, we find the key.

With every smile a shining spark,
In sharing love, we light the dark.
In kindness shown, a warmth impart,
In grateful moments, we play our part.

The little things, they matter most,
In shared blessings, we proudly boast.
With open arms, we welcome grace,
In glowing hearts, we find our place.

In evening prayers, our voices blend,
In thankful hearts, the joy won't end.
With every heartbeat, we trust and guide,
In the glow of gratitude, we abide.

Rich Tapestry of Joy

Threads of laughter interlace,
In every moment, we find our place.
With colors vibrant, life we weave,
In tapestry bright, we choose to believe.

Each joyful thread tells a tale,
In memories made, we will not fail.
Through ups and downs, our spirits soar,
In richness found, we ask for more.

The weft of kindness binds us tight,
In shared happiness, we take flight.
With every stitch, we build our dream,
In this joyful weave, we are a team.

A tapestry formed by love and grace,
In unity found, we embrace the space.
With open hearts, we spread our wings,
In the rich tapestry, joy softly sings.

The Serenade of the Stars

The night whispers softly, a melody bright,
With diamonds that twinkle, a dance in the light.
Each note floats like petals, on winds that embrace,
A serenade sings, in the vastness of space.

The moon shines like silver, a beacon so clear,
Guiding the dreamers who wander near.
In the silence, a symphony plays,
In the heart of the cosmos, lost in a gaze.

Across the expanse, where the galaxies weave,
Stories of starlight in shadows believe.
In the tapestry woven, a tale long and grand,
The serenade echoes through the twilight land.

With each gentle flicker, a wish finds its way,
Carried by stardust that sweeps through the sway.
So let the night cradle your hopes and your fears,
In the serenade of the stars, we find our prayers.

A Journey Through Sunny Days

Golden rays break through, painting all in gold,
Every moment glimmers, a story unfolds.
Laughter weaves through air, as kids run and play,
Together we wander, through sunny-filled days.

The rustle of leaves, whispers sweet to the ear,
Nature's soft chorus, a song we hold dear.
Fields full of flowers, in colors so bright,
A journey awaits in the warm morning light.

With each step we take, let our spirits run free,
The world is alive, as we soak in the glee.
Moments turn magical, in the sun's warm embrace,
A journey through sunny days, time slows its pace.

Under the vast sky, we dance without care,
Memories made in the warmth we all share.
Through laughter and whispers, we find our own way,
In this journey of joy, where the heart wants to stay.

Joy's Wandering Footsteps

Upon the path of laughter, where the wildflowers bloom,
Joy's wandering footsteps chase away all gloom.
Each step is a stanza, in a song of delight,
Every twist and turn brings new dreams in sight.

Through valleys of sunshine, and hills painted green,
Joy dances around in a world so serene.
With every heartbeat, it whispers anew,
The magic of living in all that we do.

The stream sings a tune, as it bubbles and flows,
Inviting the spirit to dance with the prose.
In the arms of nature, where worries are few,
Joy wanders along, through the skies so blue.

So let your heart follow, where the laughter resides,
In the journey of joy, find the warmth it provides.
With wandering footsteps, leave the shadows behind,
Embrace every moment, let the spirit unwind.

Radiating Through the Ordinary

In the mundane moments, where beauty can hide,
Radiance glimmers, the joy deep inside.
With a smile to share, and kindness to sow,
The ordinary sparkles, in the light's gentle glow.

Through morning routines, and the hustle of days,
We find little treasures in simple pathways.
A warm cup of coffee, a book on the shelf,
Radiating joy, just being ourselves.

In laughter and chatter, in the calm of the night,
The ordinary dances, in whispers of light.
Through the trials and triumphs, in the ebb and flow,
Radiance shines brightly, everywhere we go.

So cherish the present, let your spirit be free,
In the heart of the ordinary, blissful joy we see.
With open eyes and hearts, let life's colors blend,
Radiating through the ordinary, the magic won't end.

Moonlit Dreams and Morning Glory

In the stillness of the night,
Dreams dance beneath soft light.
Whispers float on silver beams,
As dawn awakens, bright with dreams.

Morning breaks with gentle hues,
A canvas painted with fresh views.
Birds sing sweetly, skies unfold,
A new day's tale, yet to be told.

With every step, the world feels right,
Shadows fade, embraced by light.
Nature breathes, a soothing sigh,
Hope awakens, reaching high.

So let us wander, hand in hand,
Through moonlit dreams, across the land.
With morning's grace, we'll find our way,
In every moment, come what may.

Cascades of Laughter

Laughter bubbles, light and free,
Like a river, wild and free.
Echoes dance from hill to hill,
Joy cascades, a heart to fill.

In every smile, a spark ignites,
Stories shared on starry nights.
With friends gathered, moments shine,
Laughter's melody, pure divine.

Tickles and giggles fill the air,
A symphony of love and care.
Together we weave, our dreams take flight,
In cascades of laughter, pure delight.

So let your heart embrace the cheer,
For every chuckle brings us near.
In the warmth of joy, we find our place,
Cascades of laughter, love's embrace.

Radiance in Quiet Corners

In the hush of early morn,
Soft light spills where dreams are born.
Quiet corners hold their grace,
In stillness, we find our place.

Whispers of time, gentle and clear,
Moments cherished, always near.
A simple touch, a knowing gaze,
Radiance in the quiet ways.

Within the shadows, secrets hide,
A warmth that swells from deep inside.
Nature's heartbeat, soft and slow,
In quiet corners, love can grow.

So pause awhile and take a breath,
Embrace the peace that conquers death.
For in the stillness, souls will find,
Radiance that forever binds.

Kaleidoscopic Joys of Living

Colors swirl in vibrant dance,
Life unfolds in every chance.
Moments flicker, bright and bold,
Kaleidoscopic stories told.

Through laughter, tears, and whispered dreams,
Reality flows in radiant streams.
Every heartbeat, every sigh,
A tapestry of joy when nigh.

With open arms and joyful eyes,
We embrace the world, no goodbyes.
In every corner, wonders thrive,
Kaleidoscopic joys, so alive.

So let us savor, every hue,
Life's rich palette, bright and true.
In the chaos, find your song,
In kaleidoscopic joys, we belong.

Laughter in the Breeze

Children play with joyful shouts,
Their laughter dances all about.
The sun shines bright on gleeful faces,
As summer weaves its warm embraces.

The leaves they sway with gentle glee,
Whispers soft, like a melody.
In every heart, a spark ignites,
Creating joy on sunny sights.

A breeze sings sweet like lovers' tunes,
Underneath the watchful moons.
Together we shall laugh and dream,
Our spirits free, like flowing streams.

In this moment, time stands still,
With laughter echoing, hearts will fill.
Nature's gift, the purest tease,
Forever found, in laughter's breeze.

Colors of Bliss

In gardens bright with hues so bold,
Each petal tells a tale untold.
From azure skies to emerald grass,
In every shade, our worries pass.

The sunset paints with fiery rays,
A canvas filled with golden plays.
With every brush, the heart takes flight,
In colors burst, a pure delight.

The blossoms dance in sweet array,
As gentle breezes come to play.
A kaleidoscope that brings us peace,
In nature's art, our souls increase.

These colors weave a magic thread,
A tapestry where dreams are fed.
So let us bask in this lovely bliss,
As life unfolds in colors kissed.

Whispers of Contentment

In quiet moments, peace abides,
A gentle hush, where joy resides.
Among the stillness, hearts align,
With whispered dreams, so soft, divine.

The evening stars, they twinkle bright,
A serenade of silver light.
With every breath, we find our way,
In whispers sweet, we softly stay.

The world may rush, but we will pause,
Embracing life without a cause.
In the calm, our spirits grow,
Contentment blooms, when hearts feel slow.

These whispers weave a cozy spell,
In solitude, we know it well.
So let us linger, here, in peace,
In life's embrace, we find release.

Sunshine on My Soul

The morning light breaks through the trees,
A gentle warmth upon the breeze.
It touches earth with golden rays,
Awakening my heart in praise.

Each beam of light, a sweet caress,
In every moment, purest bless.
As shadows fade, my spirit soars,
With sunlight's love, the heart restores.

The vibrant blooms respond with glee,
Each petal shines, a jubilee.
In nature's arms, I feel so whole,
With every ray, it lights my soul.

So let this sunshine guide my way,
And fill my life with joy each day.
For in this light, I truly find,
A warmth that wraps and heals the mind.

Moments Wrapped in Warmth

In the quiet of the night,
Whispers dance like firelight,
Comfort found in gentle sighs,
Wrapped in love, where warmth lies.

Every smile, a soft embrace,
Time slows down, a sacred space,
Hearts together, beating strong,
In this moment, we belong.

Stars above with twinkling eyes,
Lighting paths as shadows rise,
Simple joys, a tender pause,
Finding peace in silent cause.

Hand in hand, we walk the line,
Moments like this, truly divine,
In this world, just you and me,
Wrapped in warmth, eternally.

The Glow of Kindred Souls

In the laughter shared at dawn,
Bonds grow strong like ivy's spawn,
Familiar tunes that weave and play,
Kindred spirits come what may.

Through the storms and the delight,
Shining bright like stars at night,
In each glance, a story told,
Hearts connect, a warmth to hold.

Together in this dance of fate,
Moments treasured, never late,
Glows that flicker, love's embrace,
Painting joy on every face.

In the silence, understanding found,
Kindred hearts forever bound,
Through the years, we'll light the way,
Guiding each other, come what may.

Chasing Light on Gentle Breezes

Feel the whispers in the air,
Sunlight dances without care,
On the breeze, our dreams take flight,
Chasing moments, pure delight.

Fields of gold, the wildflowers sway,
Nature's beauty, bright display,
In the laughter, breezes swell,
Secrets shared, as stories tell.

Every moment, fleeting fast,
Like a shadow, first to last,
In the sunlight, magic's glow,
Chasing light as soft winds flow.

Together, hand in hand we roam,
Finding joy, we make it home,
In this dance, our spirits free,
Chasing light, just you and me.

Bubbles of Bliss

Floating high on dreams of air,
Bubbles rising, free from care,
In each glimmer, joy revealed,
Moments pure, our hearts unsealed.

Laughter sparkles, pure delight,
Chasing bubbles, taking flight,
Colors swirl, a vibrant show,
In this wonder, love will grow.

Sunshine kisses on our skin,
As we gather, let love in,
In these bubbles, time stands still,
Blissful heart, adventurous thrill.

With each pop, a memory made,
Lives entwined, we won't trade,
In this world of blissful dreams,
Bubbles dance in sunlight's beams.

Shimmering Threads of Love

In whispers soft, our hearts align,
With every glance, a silken sign.
The warmth of hands, a gentle touch,
Threads of love woven, mean so much.

In laughter shared beneath the stars,
Together we dance, forgetting scars.
Each moment precious, a fleeting thread,
In the tapestry of dreams we've spread.

Through storms and calm, we hold on tight,
Shimmering threads in the dark of night.
Binding our souls in a sacred weave,
In this grand tale, together we believe.

With every heartbeat, a promise graced,
In the fabric of love, we are embraced.
Through time's passage, we still remain,
Shimmering threads, a sweet refrain.

The Essence of Blissful Living

In morning light, the world awakes,
With every breath, the spirit shakes.
The essence flows in vibrant hues,
As life unfolds, we chase our muse.

In laughter's echo, joy is found,
With loving eyes, we share the sound.
In simple moments, peace we find,
The essence of living, gentle and kind.

A sunset paints the sky with grace,
In nature's arms, we find our place.
With grateful hearts, we rise and shine,
In every heartbeat, our souls entwine.

Each day a gift, a fleeting chance,
In every glance, a sacred dance.
The essence lingers, sweet and bright,
In blissful living, we find our light.

The Brightness of Togetherness

In unity, we stand so strong,
With every heartbeat, we belong.
The brightness glows in simple ways,
Together we weave our sunny days.

With hands entwined, we face the storms,
In laughter shared, our spirit warms.
Through trials faced, we find our light,
In togetherness, all wrongs feel right.

In quiet moments, we find our peace,
Embracing love that will never cease.
With every smile, our worries fade,
In the brightness of us, joy is made.

So let us cherish this bond so true,
In every dream, I'll walk with you.
Together we shine, like stars above,
In the bright embrace of endless love.

A Daydream Wrapped in Color

In hues of pastel, we drift away,
Riding on clouds in the light of day.
A daydream blooms with every thought,
In strokes of color, our hopes are caught.

With whispers soft, the colors blend,
In fields of wonder, we choose to spend.
Each brush of light, a tale unfolds,
In the canvas of dreams, our story told.

The laughter rings in vibrant sound,
In every shade, our hearts are bound.
Through golden rays and sapphire skies,
A daydream wrapped, where magic lies.

So let us wander, hand in hand,
In this world of color, so beautifully planned.
In daydreams bright, we find our way,
Wrapped in love, we forever stay.

Lightness in Laughter

In the glow of the sun, we meet,
Laughter dances on light feet.
Giggles echo through the air,
Joy ignites without a care.

With friends beside, our spirits soar,
Every jest opens a door.
In these moments, time stands still,
A simple joy, a cherished thrill.

We find delight in little things,
In the warmth that friendship brings.
Hearts entwined in gentle play,
We paint our world in bright array.

Each chuckle a melody sweet,
A life balanced on playful beat.
Together in this joyous trance,
We embrace life's whimsical dance.

Moments of Pure Elation

In the hush before the dawn,
Hope ignites the world we've drawn.
With a smile, the day begins,
Promise whispers, soft as sin.

In every heartbeat, dreams collide,
With open arms, we cast aside.
Chasing suns on paths unknown,
Together we have truly grown.

Every laugh, a spark, a light,
Chasing shadows, banishing night.
With you, dear friend, I am alive,
In this moment, we shall thrive.

Through the trials, we stand tall,
In unity, we shall not fall.
A symphony of joy and grace,
In our tender, cherished space.

Blossoms of Blissful Days

In gardens where the wildflowers bloom,
Joy cascades, dispelling gloom.
Colors burst with fragrant cheer,
Each petal whispers, 'Come near.'

Moments captured in nature's frame,
Sunshine bathed, we feel the same.
With laughter ringing through the trees,
Time unwinds gently, like a breeze.

Dancing shadows, the world alive,
In these days, our dreams survive.
With every step on this soft earth,
We celebrate the magic of birth.

Hand in hand, our spirits fly,
Underneath the endless sky.
In every smile, a story told,
In blissful days, our hearts unfold.

The Heat of Kindred Spirits

In the warmth of close embrace,
Two souls unite, a sacred space.
With every laugh, a flicker bright,
Together we ignite the night.

Through shared glances, secrets bloom,
Like fireflies lighting up the gloom.
We find our rhythm, hearts in tune,
Lost in the magic of the moon.

Winds of change may blow our way,
But together, we will stay.
In the dance of spirits near,
We forge our path, casting fear.

Through thicker bonds, we will ascend,
In unity, we shall not bend.
The heat of kindred hearts entwined,
In love's embrace, forever blind.

Glimmers of Joy

In the morning light, they shine,
Tiny sparks that intertwine.
Whispers soft upon the breeze,
Waking hearts with gentle ease.

In laughter shared and games we play,
Moments bright, they light our way.
Like stars that twinkle in the night,
Glimmers of joy, forever bright.

With every hug and caring glance,
We find reason to rejoice and dance.
In simple things, our treasures lie,
In glimmers found, we learn to fly.

So hold them close, these fleeting beams,
In life's embrace, ignite our dreams.
For joy, it lingers, waits to bloom,
In every heart, dispelling gloom.

A Symphony of Smiles

With a sparkle and a gleam,
Each smile we share, a tiny beam.
Harmony in laughter's blend,
A symphony that knows no end.

Through crowded streets or quiet nooks,
In every glance, in every book.
The world sings sweet with rhythmic grace,
When we offer each other a warm embrace.

In moments brief and memories vast,
Each smile, a note, in the present cast.
Together we weave this joyful tune,
Underneath the silver moon.

So let your smile, like music flow,
Creating warmth, letting kindness glow.
Together we'll build this melody,
In smiles, we find our harmony.

Embracing the Sunlight

Awake with the dawn, the world aglow,
Embracing the sunlight, soft and low.
The warmth upon our skin, divine,
Guiding our hearts through cheer and shine.

With each ray that pierces the trees,
Nature whispers secrets in the breeze.
Colors dance in radiant hues,
Painting the day with vibrant views.

Let shadows fade with each new day,
As sunlight kisses doubts away.
In golden fields, our spirits run,
We celebrate life beneath the sun.

So lift your face, let worries cease,
In sunlight's grasp, we find our peace.
Together we'll wander, hand in hand,
Embracing warmth, in this bright land.

The Dance of Delight

In twilight's glow, together we spin,
The dance of delight, let the joy begin.
With every step, we let worries sway,
In rhythm and laughter, we find our way.

Round and round, hand in hand,
Twisting and twirling, as dreams expand.
The world melts away, in this charmed trance,
As hearts take flight in a joyous dance.

Each laugh a note in an endless song,
Where every heartbeat feels right, not wrong.
We leap, we glide, in jubilant air,
A dance of delight, our spirits laid bare.

So come join the circle, let's celebrate,
In this dance of life, we create our fate.
For every moment, a spark to ignite,
Together we'll joyfully dance through the night.

The Playful Song of the Soul

In shadows where laughter calls,
Whispers of joy softly fall.
A dance in the gentle breeze,
The heart finds its playful keys.

With every beat, the spirit sings,
Unfurling the joy that life brings.
Through laughter and light, we roam,
Eternal, our playful home.

In dreams where the starlight glows,
The melody of freedom flows.
Each step is a story told,
A tapestry woven in gold.

Embrace the song that won't fade,
In each moment, memories made.
For in the heart's joyful quest,
We find our soul's sweetest rest.

Whimsical Trails of Delight

Upon the path where wonders bloom,
In every corner, magic's loom.
A giggle from the flowers bright,
Whispers tales of pure delight.

The sun drapes warmth on every face,
As we wander, lost in grace.
With butterflies that dance and play,
Life's wonders unfold each day.

Through fields where dreams and colors blend,
Every moment, our hearts transcend.
A secret path of laughter flows,
In the breeze, a soft hope glows.

So let us stroll this cheerful ground,
Where joy abounds and love is found.
With every step, the joy ignites,
In whimsical trails of endless nights.

Embracing Euphoria

In the arms of nature's grace,
We find our breath, our sacred space.
With open hearts, we rise and soar,
Embracing euphoria evermore.

Each sunrise paints a new delight,
Hope ignites with morning light.
With laughter shared, we feel alive,
In unity, we learn to thrive.

Through tempests fierce, we hold our ground,
In dreams, the strength of love is found.
With every challenge, courage grows,
In euphoria, our spirit glows.

So let us dance beneath the stars,
Free from worries and all our scars.
For in this moment, we are whole,
Embracing bliss within our soul.

The Palette of Pure Bliss

With colors bright, our hearts ignite,
Each hue a dream taking flight.
From golden dawn to twilight's kiss,
We paint our lives with pure bliss.

The skies erupt in shades of glee,
A canvas wild, forever free.
In every stroke, we find a way,
To capture joy in each day.

Let laughter splash like vibrant paint,
In life's great art, our fears grow faint.
The palette swirls, emotions rise,
In every color, love belies.

So blend your shades, let worries cease,
In the masterpiece of inner peace.
For happiness is ours to find,
In the palette of a loving mind.

Blooming Hearts in Full Color

In gardens where the flowers sway,
Hearts unravel, bright and gay.
Petals whisper, secrets sigh,
Color blooms as dreams fly high.

Sunlight kisses every hue,
Nature's canvas, rich and true.
Joyful laughter fills the air,
In this beauty, love we share.

The Dance of Cheerful Spirits

In fields where shadows play and gleam,
Spirits swirl, a joyful dream.
With every step, the world's alive,
In this dance, our hearts will thrive.

Laughter twinkles, eyes aglow,
Together, we let happiness flow.
Fingers entwined, we twirl around,
In this moment, pure joy is found.

Glistening Moments of Delight

Every drop of dew that clings,
Holds the joy that morning brings.
Glistening leaves, a sparkling show,
Nature's treasure, a gentle glow.

In fleeting seconds, wonder waits,
Each moment quickly captivates.
See the world through eyes so bright,
Glistening moments, pure delight.

A Symphony of Sunshine

Radiant beams on morning's crest,
Nature plays its sweetest jest.
Each ray a note, each breeze a song,
In this symphony, we belong.

Golden hues paint skies so wide,
In the warmth, our hopes reside.
With open hearts, we sing along,
In this harmony, we are strong.

Glimmering Pathways of Joy

In the morning light so bright,
Joy dances on the leaves' green flight.
Footsteps guide us through this way,
Glimmering pathways, come what may.

Laughter echoes in the air,
Moments shared, so light, so rare.
Every smile a shining star,
Leading us to who we are.

Nature sings a joyful tune,
Underneath the silver moon.
Hearts entwined in blissful dreams,
Life unfolds in golden beams.

Together we will roam and play,
In glimmering pathways, come what may.
Holding hands through thick and thin,
With every step, we truly win.

Hearts Ablaze in Togetherness

In the warmth where shadows blend,
Hearts ablaze, our souls ascend.
Unified in every glance,
Together we embrace the chance.

Fires of passion gently blaze,
Guiding us through life's maze.
Side by side, we stand so tall,
In togetherness, we have it all.

Through laughter and the tears we share,
We find strength beyond compare.
Connected souls, forever bound,
In every heartbeat, love is found.

With every moment, love ignites,
Hearts ablaze, our spirits light.
In you, my joy, my heart's delight,
Together we embrace the night.

Joy's Gentle Serenade

A soft whisper in the breeze,
Joy's serenade, a sweet tease.
In every note, a gentle sway,
Life's music calls us every day.

Sunset paints the evening sky,
As laughter twinkles, soft and shy.
Moments captured, sweet and rare,
In joy's embrace, we lay bare.

Every heartbeat sings a song,
In this unity, we belong.
Life's sweet rhythm as we glide,
In joy's gentle arms, we confide.

So let us dance beneath the stars,
With joy as our guide, no borders, no bars.
The world our stage, together we sway,
In joy's serenade, come what may.

The Sweetness of Easy Laughter

In the daylight's tender glow,
Laughter bubbles, soft and low.
Shared glances, with smiles so wide,
In each moment, joy's our guide.

Playful banter fills the air,
With easy laughter, troubles rare.
Every chuckle breaks the night,
Turning shadows into light.

Like a melody, it flows,
In the heart, the laughter grows.
Simple moments, pure delight,
In the warmth, we feel so right.

So let us savor every cheer,
The sweetness of laughter, crystal clear.
In this dance of joy and play,
Easy laughter leads the way.